Klatt's June '94

W9-CCD-750

SOLVING FLATWORK PROBLEMS

by

Jane Wallace

Illustrations by

Carole Vincer

THRESHOLD BOOKS

First published in Great Britain by
Threshold Books, The Kenilworth Press Limited,
Addington, Buckingham, MK18 2JR

© The Kenilworth Press Limited 1993

All rights reserved. No part of this publication may
be reproduced, stored in a retrieval system, or
transmitted in any form or by any means, electronic,
mechanical, photocopying, recording or otherwise,
without the written permission of the publisher.

British Library Cataloguing in Publication Data
A catalogue record for this book is available from the British Library.

ISBN 1-872082-43-2

Typeset by The Kenilworth Press Limited

Printed in Great Britain by Westway Offset, Wembley

CONTENTS

Introduction

Before trying to solve any flatwork problems it is important to know what the aim of training a horse should be. The object is to produce a well-balanced, supple horse who has a good mouth and is totally obedient to the aids. Obedience in a horse can be enjoyed in whatever he does, whether it be competing or just hacking out. It is also important to understand why a horse reacts in a particular way and how a problem should be tackled to prevent it from recurring.

Resisting is a word which appears all too often on a dressage sheet. A horse may resist in many different ways but fundamentally he is disobeying his rider's aids. A horse may resist something which he finds difficult or does not understand. The rider's task is to school his horse so that the horse can obey his rider without resistance. Basic and thorough schooling as described in *Flatwork Exercises* (also in this series) should produce an obedient, supple, well-balanced horse. The horse must be given time to develop and strengthen muscles necessary for working at the required level.

A horse who finds his work easy will be easy to train. If he finds something difficult he will resist and this resistance will depend upon his character. Each horse is an individual and will react in a different way.

The root cause of many problems can be found in the animal's conformation; e.g. a badly put together horse will be unable to carry himself in balance; a horse with poor paces will find it impossible to keep a good rhythm; a short, bull-necked horse will find it difficult to work in a round shape.

Throughout the text the words **horse** and **pony** are interchangeable - the advice applies equally to both.

If you have a difficult horse or pony, or are experiencing persistent problems, seek the advice of a professional.

Tenseness and excitability

If a horse is tense it suggests that he is unhappy about something: he could be anxious about the rider or what he is being asked to do; he could be somewhere exciting or alarming; he could just be fresh and exuberant; or he could be in discomfort from, say, the bit, the saddle or the weight of the rider.

An excited, fresh horse should be ridden strongly forward (perhaps with a finger in the neckstrap for safety) and given work to do which gives him other things to think about. It is often in a new environment that a horse reacts in an excitable manner. He may associate the place with galloping and jumping, or he may be a young horse unused to outside stimuli. The horse has to be given time to settle before he can be expected to concentrate and work sensibly. He must be allowed to 'let off steam' by doing some vigorous trot and canter work. It is sometimes advisable to put the horse on the lunge to allow him to get rid of his high spirits. This way you do not need to worry about being bucked off - but make sure someone strong is on the end of the lunge line.

With a tense horse, try to find the reason for his anxiety. If he is reacting to discomfort try to remove the cause, e.g. change to a milder bit, or to a different saddle with better protection for the back. Try sitting more lightly on your horse.

If your horse is persistently tense it is worth asking your veterinary surgeon to check him for physical problems.

A good way to settle a horse is to work him on a long rein, making him stretch down and so relax his muscles. Once the horse is physically relaxed he can then relax mentally.

Make sure that *you* are relaxed too.

Not going forward

This is a fundamental problem and occurs in all newly broken horses. A horse has to learn to go forwards and needs a reason for wanting to do so.

The problem may be found in a lazy horse, and can be induced by a rider trying to 'collect' the horse in the wrong way, i.e. from the front. The rider should always ride the horse from behind into his hand, and not just pull in the horse's head.

With a green horse who has no reason to go forward, strong encouraging riding plus plenty of hacking out in company should help the horse understand the meaning of forward movement.

A horse who ignores his rider's leg must be taught respect. He must learn that when the rider applies his leg with a squeeze, he must respond. The way to teach the horse to answer the leg is to apply the leg with a squeeze and if the horse does not move forward immediately, give him a sharp kick. If the horse still ignores the leg, the rider should give him a flick with a schooling whip (always take the hand off the rein when using a whip other than a schooling whip). It may be necessary to wear spurs to make some horses take notice of the leg. However, it is not a good idea to wear spurs all the time because the horse may become immune to them, and it is advisable to have an extra aid when riding in a competition.

Always ride the horse into a contact and remember that the horse must take the contact from the rider, not vice versa. You should feel that your horse is ready to move up a pace at any time and is responsive to the slightest leg aid. Aim for invisible aids!

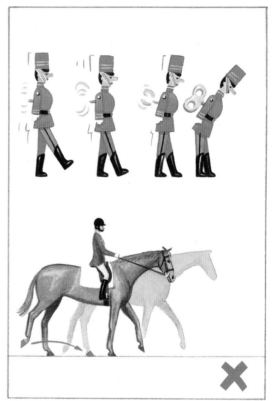

The horse must take positive steps and not be like a clockwork toy running down.

Laziness

Some horses and ponies are bone idle! They pretend not to understand the rider's aids and as a result the rider tends to end up nagging with the leg. It is a common sight to see a rider monotonously kicking the horse on every stride and the horse not taking the slightest notice.

A horse may appear to be lazy when in fact he is unfit or unwell. A fat, unfit pony living on grass is less likely to have the same energy as a fit, stabled pony. From lack of fitness comes lethargy and an unwillingness for exertion.

If you think that your horse is ailing, ask your veterinary surgeon to examine him and perhaps carry out a blood test to check for the presence of a virus.

If lack of fitness is causing the laziness, aim to get your horse fitter and give him a higher energy diet to improve performance.

A naturally lazy horse must be taught to respect the rider's leg in the same way as a horse who does not go forwards. A whip or a pair of spurs can be used as artificial aids to reinforce the leg aid until the horse learns that he must react to a squeeze.

Some ponies react to the whip by bucking or kicking out. They must learn that this behaviour is not acceptable, and you should seek professional help. The horse must be taught to respect a flick from the whip in the same way as he respects the leg.

A lazy horse is easier to cope with than an excitable one. You can soon galvanise a horse into action - but it is more difficult to calm one down.

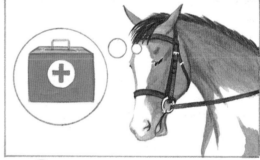

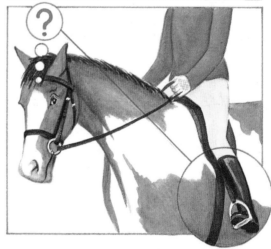

Crookedness

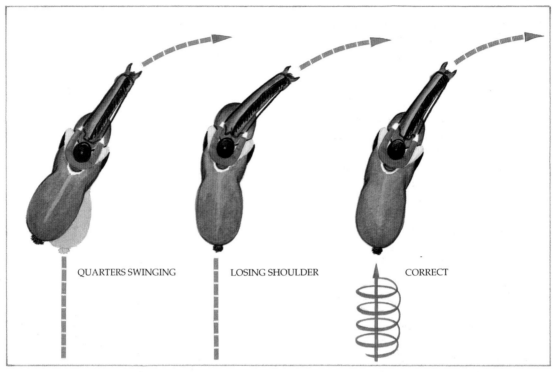

QUARTERS SWINGING   LOSING SHOULDER   CORRECT

A horse is said to be straight when the hind feet follow the track made by the forefeet. The horse's feet are rather like the wheels on an electric train - if the wheels come off one track, the train is derailed.

In order for the horse to stay on one track on the corners, he must bend through his body to allow this to happen. If the horse is stiff, his quarters will swing or he will fall in. When working on the straight the quarters sometimes trace a different track and this is when the horse is said to be crooked.

When riding in a school, the wall or fence will help to keep the horse straight. When working in an open field with no fence to guide the horse it is more difficult to keep him straight.

Some horses like to carry themselves perpetually crooked. This may mean they have a problem in the back and are compensating by moving away from the discomfort. A veterinary surgeon can diagnose this for you.

Horses often canter crookedly to help their balance: to avoid bringing his hocks underneath him the horse swings his quarters to the inside instead.

A common fault when coming up the centre line is for the horse to carry his quarters to one side, and this is all the more apparent when the horse halts. The rider should always correct this problem by aligning the forehand with the hindquarters and should not try to straighten up by moving the hindquarters.

Sending the horse forward more vigorously will also help to straighten him in the same way that pedalling faster stops a bicycle wobbling. Although the horse must learn to move away from the leg, the leg should basically mean move forwards. Two-track aids must be specific.

Shortening stride

Some horses naturally move better than others. The horse who takes shorter strides when ridden than when loose or on the lunge is evading work by not working enough from behind.

Short steps may be caused by the horse not going forward or by restriction from the rider. The horse will be pulling himself along on his forehand with little or no propulsion from behind. He will have difficulty in keeping a rhythm and will be unlikely to take an even contact on the rein.

It may be that the horse is tense or excited or is unhappy in his back or mouth. If the ground is hard it is worth considering whether your horse is jarred up or has a problem with his feet. Seek professional advice if the problem persists.

When trying to improve this problem it is important to re-establish the basics of calmness and forward movement. Once these are established the rider should aim to make his horse as supple as possible so that he is less likely to lose rhythm on corners.

The more supple the horse, the looser his movement will become. All paces are affected if the horse is stiff. Working on a long rein with plenty of circles and changes of rein will help to supple the horse, encourage him to work from behind and push evenly with his hocks. The rider should aim to ride on the lightest of contacts so that the horse can carry himself and not feel any restriction that may shorten his stride.

In most instances of horses not striding out it is a lack of balance that affects it most. If a horse is not balanced his hocks will be trailing and inactive, creating minimum drive or push from behind.

Lack of balance means shorter stride

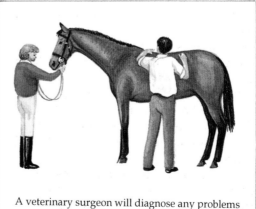

A veterinary surgeon will diagnose any problems

Running through the rider's hand

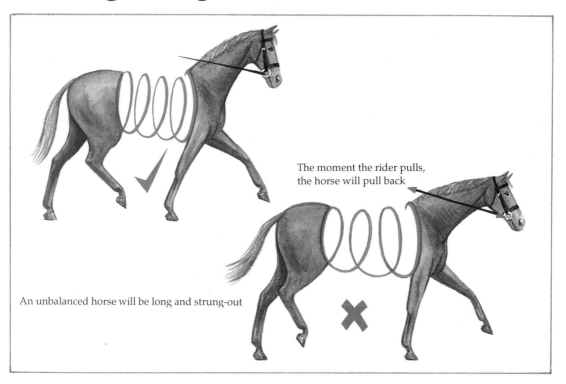

The moment the rider pulls, the horse will pull back

An unbalanced horse will be long and strung-out

This is when the rider closes his leg and then his hand, and the horse ignores the hand and keeps going. Unless the horse responds to the hand he will not alter his shape by lightening his forehand and lowering his hindquarters. An unbalanced horse will be long and strung-out.

Some horses are naturally better balanced and able to carry themselves due to their conformation. Others require more training to achieve the same result. It is vital that the impulsion created by the rider's legs can be contained, otherwise the horse will never progress in his training and will remain on the forehand.

A series of half-halts and lots of transitions are the methods of improving this particular problem. Repeating transitions will help teach the horse to adjust his balance without having to use his rider's hand.

When making a downward transition the rider should close his legs, stretch his spine and then close his hand. If the horse resists the hand, the rider should keep the leg closed and give and take a little with his hand, maybe moving the bit gently in the horse's mouth. On no account should the rider pull - the moment the rider pulls, the horse will pull back.

A series of half-halts may be necessary to establish a pace if a horse is unbalanced and strong. The rider should close his leg and use a blocking hand followed by a light hand as a reward when the horse responds.

It may be necessary to use a stronger noseband or bit if the rider is not strong enough to hold the horse. This is more likely in an older horse who is set in his ways.

Stiffness

If a horse is to bend around his corners or bring his hocks under him he must be supple, particularly in the muscles along his back. When you read 'stiff' on a dressage sheet, it refers to lack of suppleness, which does not permit the horse to carry out the specific movements in the test. If a horse is stiff in his back he will avoid bending round corners and will hollow his outline.

Stiffness is caused by a lack of training or possibly a physical defect in the back. A short-backed horse will find it more difficult to bend than one with a longer back because his back will be naturally more rigid.

Suppleness is an important requirement in the athletic horse and all training is geared towards producing a supple, elastic horse. The horse must be given sufficient time to warm up before a schooling session and, similarly, time to cool off afterwards. This avoids damaging muscles by working them before they are ready.

A stiff horse will have many inter-related problems such as an inability to keep a rhythm and carry himself in true balance.

Suppling a horse takes time and involves hours of hard work, practising bending and stretching exercises such as circles, changes of direction, serpentines, decreasing and increasing circles, transitions, shoulder-in and trotting poles. Do not be tempted to work the horse for too long, though. If he becomes tired, he will be stiffer and the problem will be made worse. Try not to sit heavily - feel that you 'kiss' the saddle in rising trot and avoid sitting trot until the horse is stronger in his back.

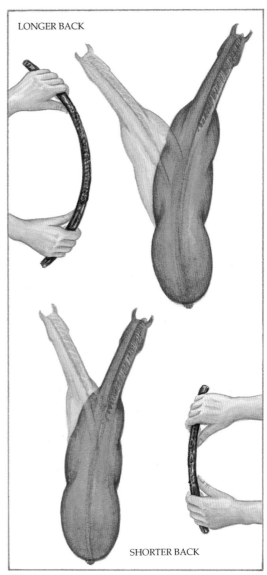

LONGER BACK

SHORTER BACK

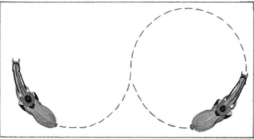

Falling in

Instead of tracking true (with the hind feet following the front feet), the horse does not bend around the rider's inside leg and moves onto two tracks. It may be caused by stiffness or by the horse shying at something. It stems from a basic lack of training and obedience. The horse must learn to move from the inside leg. The rider should work on suppling exercises.

It is a common sight to see ponies 'motor-biking' round their corners in a dressage arena. As they fall in round the corners there is a loss of rhythm and balance and the whole test is spoilt.

Balance is all-important when going round a corner. The horse finds his balance from taking the weight on his inside hind leg. All movements require preparation and each corner should be set up well in advance. The rider should ask the horse for a bend at the quarter marker before the corner. The inside hand asks for the horse to flex at the jaw, and the inside leg engages the inside hind leg and asks for the bend. The outside rein controls the shoulder and allows the horse to bend, and the outside leg prevents the quarters from swinging out. The most 'active' aids are the inside ones - the outside aids are ready to prevent evasion.

If a horse falls in despite the rider giving clear aids, an open rein may be used. The rider asks for the bend before the corner, with the inside aids; he then takes his outside hand towards the school wall, or to the outside, to guide the horse into the corner. The horse cannot then fall in. This schooling remedy will help, but the rider must aim to teach the horse to respond and be obedient to the inside leg.

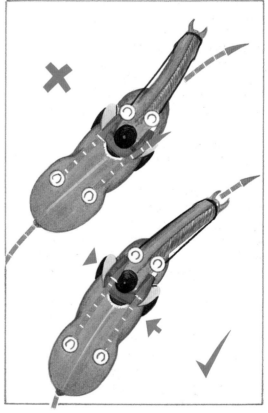

One-sidedness

Most horses are more supple one way than the other. They find it easier to perform various movements on a particular rein. The majority of problems evinced in the mouth are caused by the horse not carrying the weight evenly on his hocks. The degree of suppleness on a corner depends on how much the horse can flex through his ribs and bring his inside hock underneath him. Any stiffness here shows up in the horse's mouth.

A horse which has been injured in a hind limb, or has a weakness, will be stiff in his mouth on that side. Any problems in the back will also show up through lack of response in the mouth.

A horse with tooth problems may be one-sided. The cause could be sharp teeth (molars) in need of rasping, or wolf teeth* which require removal. Ask your veterinary surgeon to check your horse's teeth every six months.

A sore mouth or cracked, split corners will cause the horse to be one-sided. A horse will always try to go away from pain so will resist turning to the side on which his mouth is sore.

You could lunge your horse or ride him in a bitless bridle to give his mouth time to heal.

It is important that the rider is aware that his horse is heavier in one hand than the other. If a horse learns that he can lean on one hand, he will continue to do so. A one-sided horse can make a rider permanently heavier in one hand, so beware!

Concentrate on suppling exercises, working more on the stiff rein but avoid over-tiring the horse on that side.

* Wolf teeth are small, shallow-rooted teeth which grow in front of the upper, and very occasionally the lower, molars and interfere with the action of the bit.

There is a different response to the rider's hand on the horse's good rein, and on his stiff side

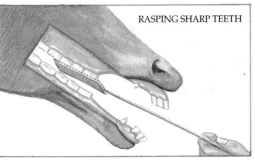

RASPING SHARP TEETH

Leaning/On the forehand

When the horse leans, he is relying on the rider's hand for his balance instead of using his hocks. The rider has a heavy feeling in his hand as if he is supporting the horse - he is!

In order for the forehand to be light, the hindquarters must lower. The horse is like a see-saw in this respect. Conformation plays a large part in a horse being able to balance himself naturally. Most horses take a long time to adjust to the rider's weight and it takes years for them to be able to carry themselves with ease and efficiency.

A young horse will almost certainly be on his forehand until he learns to balance himself. During this learning process it is important that the rider does not allow the horse to find that balance on his hand. The horse must learn to find his own carriage. General schooling exercises will help to improve the balance and teach the horse to use his hocks.

An older horse who has learnt to lean on his rider's hand has to be re-schooled to improve him. Any movements which increase the engagement of the hocks, such as transitions, half-halts, turns and circles, and work over trotting poles, will help. If the horse tries to lean during these exercises, the rider should use a series of strong half-halts to prevent the horse running through the hand. It may help to change the bit. A fixed mouth snaffle such as an eggbutt or Fulmer should be avoided, while a loose-ring snaffle (or in severe cases a roller snaffle) will prevent the horse from fixing on the bit. The horse must understand that the rider is no longer going to allow him to use his hand for balance.

The balance needs to be readjusted with the weight transferred to the hindquarters, so lightening the forehand

Overbending

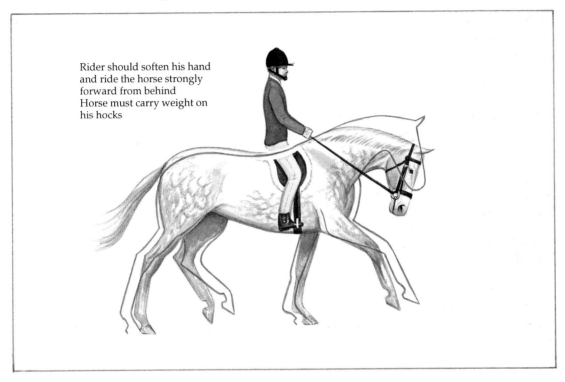

Rider should soften his hand and ride the horse strongly forward from behind
Horse must carry weight on his hocks

Here the horse's nose comes behind the vertical in his profile. In consequence the horse may drop the contact or become very strong. Both are caused by the horse not taking enough weight on his hindquarters and so losing balance. A horse may be forced into being overbent by a rider with heavy hands. If the rider does not soften his hands when the horse relaxes his jaw, the horse is made to come behind the vertical although he may not drop behind the contact.

In all instances, the rider should soften his hand and ride the horse strongly forward from behind. The horse should be encouraged to stretch down onto a contact. Working on a long (not loose) rein should help achieve this. The rider should always remember that it is the horse who should take the contact from the rider, not the other way round. If the rider bears this in mind when schooling, he should avoid falling into the trap of being too strong in the hand.

A horse who pulls with his nose tucked in can be difficult to cure. The rider should soften his hand, close the leg and then close the hand. This is (in effect) a half-halt, and by using a series of these the rider should be able to transfer some of the weight from the forehand to the rear.

A light-mouthed horse is more prone to this form of evasion than a heavier, less-responsive type of horse. A horse who refuses to take a contact and is behind the bit is one of the most difficult to improve. You cannot make a horse take a contact but unless he does he can never be truly between hand and leg.

It is often difficult to feel when a horse is overbent, and this is when someone on the ground is useful.

Pulling

A horse may pull for a variety of reasons. He may be fresh and exuberant, eager to get on with his job, or he may be running away from discomfort. A horse lacking in balance will also give the rider the feeling that he is pulling: as the horse relies on the rider's hand for his balance, the rider will have a heavy feeling which can be mistaken for pulling. Actually such a horse is leaning (see previous section).

There is a great temptation to give a horse who pulls a good yank to stop him, but this rarely works. The horse will merely become upset and the situation will worsen. Remember the old saying, 'It takes two to pull'. If you pull back at the horse, a vicious circle will ensue.

An excited horse will stop pulling once he has settled down. The undisciplined horse who pulls from habit has to learn that he cannot continue to hang on his rider's hand. The only way to lighten a heavy forehand is to use a series of half-halts and plenty of transitions to teach the horse that he must take the weight on his hindquarters, not on his forehand.

During the half-halts, the horse will probably try to run through the rider's hand (see earlier section). You must close the leg and then close the hand until the horse goes at the pace you want, and then you can soften the hand. You will have to repeat this until the horse understands - it will require patience.

A horse may run from pain in his back or mouth. Sometimes, by changing to a milder bit, the horse relaxes and pulls less. Back pain and mouth problems can be diagnosed by your veterinary surgeon.

A common problem caused by a pulling horse is for the rider to end up balancing on his horse's mouth - a bit like water-skiing!

A horse may pull if he is fresh or excited ...

... or he may be in discomfort

Hollow

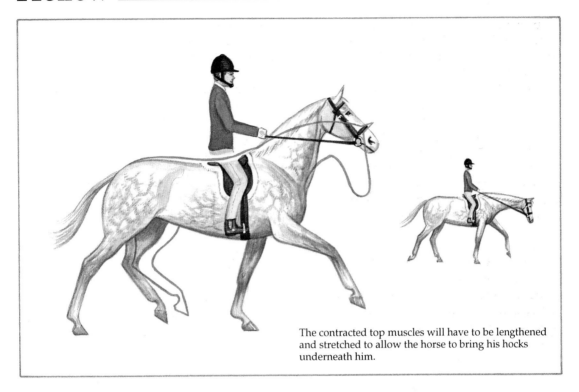

The contracted top muscles will have to be lengthened and stretched to allow the horse to bring his hocks underneath him.

A hollow outline indicates that the horse is above the bit with a stiff back and restricted neck. If he has been working in this way for some time, he will be incorrectly muscled. He will lack muscles on his top line - i.e. along his back, neck and quarters - and will probably have a bulge of muscle under his neck. This is a sign of incorrect training, although some horses' conformation predisposes this fault.

The contracted top muscles will have to be lengthened and stretched to allow the horse to bring his hocks underneath him. He will require time and plenty of suppling exercises to change his natural outline.

Work on a long rein, with the horse working long and low, is beneficial. This, coupled with basic schooling exercises such as circles, serpentines, transitions, trotting poles and increases and decreases of pace, will help to improve suppleness in the horse's back.

Do not forget that if a horse has been used to carrying himself 'upside-down' his muscles will be unused to working in a different way. It is important not to induce muscle damage by asking the horse to do too much too soon. Like any athlete, the horse must be given time to build up muscles and supple those which have not been worked correctly.

A hollow back is a weak back and therefore more likely to strain. If a horse works in a hollow outline on the flat, he is bound to jump hollow and so lack athleticism. It is important to establish the correct shape when training a horse, right from the very beginning. Problems such as this one should be avoided from the start.

Crossing jaw

The horse crosses his jaw to evade the action of the bit. He tries to relieve the pressure from the bit and his rider's hand by moving his jaw from one side to the other. When there is no contact, the horse is unlikely to cross his jaw because there is nothing to resist.

If a horse crosses his jaw as soon as the bit is put in his mouth it suggests that he finds the bit itself uncomfortable. In this case it is worth trying different bits until you find one that is suitable. Some horses hate the nutcracker action of a snaffle and prefer the double joint of a French-link snaffle.

A sore mouth, caused by sharp teeth for example, will give the horse reason to resent the pressure of the bit in his mouth. It is important to rule out these possibilities before taking further action.

Any resistance in the mouth is caused mainly by lack of balance or engagement of the hocks. It is when the horse looks to the hand for support that he finds a stronger contact, and then resists. If the horse works from his hocks, the contact need change little.

General suppling and schooling exercises will help improve balance and hock engagement. A noseband such as a grakle, a flash or a drop will help prevent the horse from opening his mouth (but it should not be so tight that it keeps the mouth shut). By using a restrictive type of noseband which discourages the horse from crossing his jaw, the horse can be taught to work better from behind. A noseband is merely a deterrent and it depends on the individual horse as to which noseband is most effective.

A change of noseband can help.

Faulty canter strike-off

Some horses are difficult about striking off on a particular lead. The aids given must be clear and the horse well prepared for the transition. To ask a horse to move from trot to canter the rider should (from sitting trot), make a half-halt before a corner, make sure there is a correct bend, and then with the outside leg behind the girth (it should be there anyway on a bend) ask the horse to canter with the inside leg. The rider's weight should be on the inside seat bone to help the horse's balance.

If the horse tries to trot faster, the rider should bring the horse back with a half-halt and then re-apply the canter aids, more positively this time. Similarly if the horse strikes off incorrectly, do not haul him back to trot - give a correct aid and try again.

A horse will fall out with his shoulder when he evades cantering on one lead. The rider must use enough outside hand to prevent this. Try changing from the horse's good rein to his difficult one and as you change direction, ask for canter strike-off.

It is often easier to make a horse canter on his less-favourite lead when out in the open and when riding more forward. A horse will naturally balance himself by cantering on the necessary lead. If you carry a whip, use it in the outside hand because it is the outside hind which takes the first canter step. A flick with the whip at the same time as giving the aids with the leg, often helps. If the horse falls out with his shoulder, you can tap him with the whip on the outside shoulder.

Make sure you do not lean to one side. This unbalances the horse, and makes things worse.

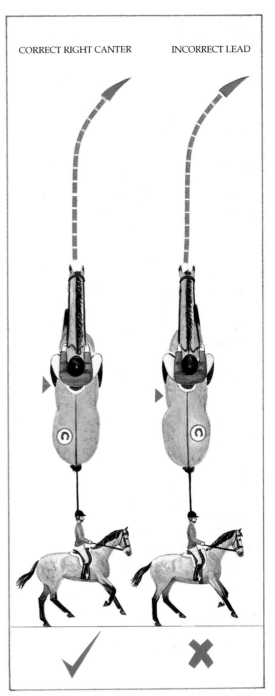

CORRECT RIGHT CANTER   INCORRECT LEAD

The outside hind takes the first canter beat

Four-time canter

Canter is a three-time movement and gallop a four-time one. A four-time canter is when the horse splits the diagonal beat, and the outside foreleg hits the ground just ahead of the inside hind. (In gallop, the diagonal is divided the other way round.) The smooth action of the canter is lost and the horse will be stiff and uncomfortable to ride. It occurs as a result of the horse not working enough from behind and not going forward. Some horses' action predisposes to cantering in this way, but more often it is caused by the rider shortening the horse too much from the front instead of driving him up from behind.

The immediate way to correct the four-time beat is to send the horse strongly forward, even slightly faster. The horse is then encouraged to push more, and so change to three beats. An effective method is to take up a forward position and send the horse into a stronger pace. The lack of weight on the saddle encourages the horse to loosen his back muscles.

Once the horse can canter well in this way, the rider can ask for some changes of pace within the canter, ensuring that the horse stays in rhythm. The moment the horse drops into four-time, the rider must send him on again.

The rider must be aware of his hand and keep it light and relaxed all the time. Any tension from the rider's hand will affect the canter and may well have caused the problem in the first place.

This is a bad habit for the horse to pick up and is not easy to cure. A horse will tend to revert easily.

Disunited canter

This is a sign that the horse is unbalanced. It is most uncomfortable for the rider and should be corrected at once. The horse may correct himself by changing, but the rider must be aware that his horse is disunited and encourage the horse to change to a true canter. A horse is unlikely to strike off into a disunited canter but will change, normally behind, so that he becomes disunited. This happens when he does not bring his outside hind well enough under him in canter, or when he swings his quarters out and loses balance. He may change in front when he is asked to change direction and fails to make a complete flying change. In a flying change the horse must simultaneously change in front and behind. If he fails to use his hocks, he will not change behind and so becomes disunited.

A rider has two options when his horse is disunited. He can preferably go back to trot and canter again, or ride his horse very strongly forward and encourage him to change. Some horses change behind from habit, caused by a weakness of one hind leg which the horse finds difficult to bring underneath him.

The rider must ensure that he keeps his outside leg firmly in position to prevent the horse from swinging outwards. It is important not to try to canter for too long at any one time. If a horse has a problem, he should canter for short bouts without becoming disunited. Once he becomes tired, he has every excuse. Cantering in the forward position helps the horse to overcome this problem, by freeing his back of weight.

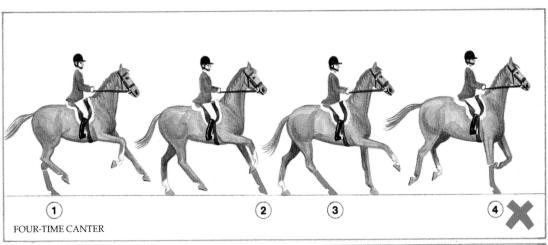

① ② ③ ④ ✖

FOUR-TIME CANTER

① ② ② ③ ✔

THREE-TIME CANTER

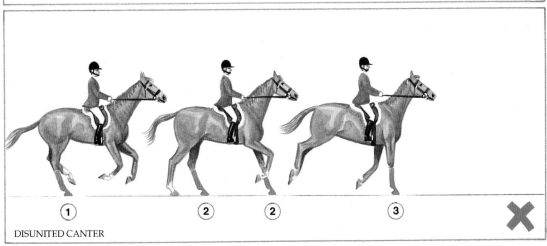

① ② ② ③ ✖

DISUNITED CANTER

Shying

Some horses are naturally more 'spooky' than others. A young horse is liable to be suspicious until he has learnt that various objects are not going to hurt him. Some older horses remain apparently terrified of things which they see every day. This attitude depends upon the character of each horse.

Some horses avoid work by shying and think it is a bit of a game, particularly when their riders become irritated. This is the worst response. If the rider gets annoyed with his horse to the extent that he perhaps loses his temper, the horse will become even more tense. He will be worried about the spooky object and about his rider. Instead, the rider should concentrate on making the horse as responsive as possible to his leg aids so that when the horse does shy, he obeys his rider rather than reacting in a disobedient way.

You should work on circles, shoulder-in, leg yield and enlarging the circle so that the horse understands the inside leg aid. Then, with the use of an indirect inside hand (inside hand taken in the direction of the rider's outside hip) and open outside rein, the horse can be prevented from moving away from the spooky object. Try giving the horse a pat and ignoring the object yourself. Avoid asking the horse to go too near it, particularly if he is fresh and feeling silly. When a horse shies, he is tense and then all sorts of other problems follow. Try to edge towards frightening objects rather than make a big issue out of them. Your horse must have confidence in you, the rider, so be firm, insist on obedience but at the same time give reassurance.

Tail swishing

This is a sign that the horse is not happy about something. It may be that he resents the rider's leg, his weight or the saddle itself. If the horse swishes his tail continually it is an ominous sign and the advice of a veterinary surgeon should be sought. In the case of a mare, it may be an ovarian cyst; or otherwise a back problem.

If the horse swishes his tail against the rider's leg, the rider should try to use a more subtle aid. Invisible aids should be the aim, and most horses do not object to a squeeze. A constantly moving lower leg (unconscious leg aid) can be very irritating for a sensitive horse. The more the horse is going forward, the less the rider needs to nag with his leg, giving the horse less reason for becoming irritable.

Check there is no discomfort beneath the girth - that there is no skin being pinched or a girth gall. Make sure that you use a thick numnah to eliminate any pinching from the saddle. The horse cannot tell us verbally that something hurts or annoys him, so we have to try to interpret other signs. The more quietly you sit and the more lightly you give the aids, the less cause the horse has to be upset.

Thin-skinned horses can be ultra-sensitive and require gentle handling. Cob types are much less tetchy and tend to be more easy-going.

Make sure that the aid you give is in the correct place and that your leg does not slide back. This can be ticklish and annoying for most horses. The fitter a horse becomes, the more sympathetic and understanding the rider needs to be for he is now dealing with a finely tuned machine.

Resents rider or rider's leg

Final thoughts

The most important aspects of training are to establish balance and rhythm and to make sure the horse is going forward with impulsion. Unless the horse is able to work with these basics, he will be unable to progress in his training and will produce problem after problem.

It is vital that the rider understands the reasons behind any resistance, because understanding a problem is halfway to curing it. Most horses will try hard in their work unless there is a good reason not to co-operate. Horses also have good memories and they rarely forget what they have learnt. It is important, therefore, that they are taught correctly in the first place. Sometimes it is convenient for them to take the easy option, which leads to bad habits. The rider must be aware of this and prevent it if possible.

Each horse is different and needs treating as an individual, yet schooling exercises are much the same for everyone. There is no magic for producing a well-schooled horse, nor are there any short-cuts. It is a case of hard work and patience.

Every horse will show some sign of resistance at some stage. The answer is to nip any bad habit in the bud and concentrate on establishing the basics as thoroughly as possible. If there are any flaws in the basic work, they will most certainly come to light as the training progresses to higher levels.

Training horses can be frustrating but mostly it is rewarding, and to produce a well-schooled horse is immensely satisfying, making all the hard work worthwhile.